MAY FREEDOM SWAY SWING

BY PE MBA UKAGWU JR.

RoseDog Books

PITTSBURGH, PENNSYLVANIA 15238

May Freedom Sway Swing is simultaneously being published in the USA and the Biafran Land.

RoseDog Books
585 Alpha Drive, Suite 103
Pittsburgh, PA 15238
Visit our website at www.rosedogbookstore.com

ISBN: 978-1-6366-1571-4
eISBN: 978-1-6366-1600-1

ABOUT THE AUTHOR: PE MBA UKAGWU JR. is a Virginian litterateur extraordinaire of Biafran extract who has written numerous books. He's an essayist, a casuistic sociologist, a poet and an exegetical pundit. He's a U.S. Marine War Veteran, a graduate student, an Associate Member of Academy of American Poets, a Member of Poetry Society of Vermont, a member of humanitarian and rights organizations. Above all, he's a devout, but struggling Christian. He lives in Chester, Pennsylvania. He loves playing and watching soccer and UFC.

FORTHCOMING BOOKS
BY PE MBA UKAGWU JR.

The Mystery of Life: The Purpose of Existence
Utilize Your Potential And Crush Problems
The Antihuman And Virtues
Ugly Truth: What We Need To Know, Not What We Want To Know
Virtues and Social Issues
African Heritage
Facts of Life: Rising Above Life's Intractable Issues (Prose-poem)
Facts of Life: Effective Relationships (Prose-poem)

POETRY:

When Love Reigns
Fractured Humanity
Rabid, Rancorous Racism
Patriots of Humanity
Denouements of Life's Mysteries
Theocentricism
Kakistocracy
Uxorial
Syncretism
Transcendental Light: Beyond Our Life
The Rape of Time
Casualties of Plutocratic System
Giant of Africa
Whatever Life Brings
Treasure of Treasures
Unfree Freedom
Bitter Divine Truth
Actualities
The Crusade

Life Undreaded
O Mankind!
Prologue & Epilogue of Life
The Provenance of Things
Into bits Things Crumble
Inner Chamber of Life
Life's Fateful Boons & Dooms
Raison D' Etre
Political Nincompoop's Paradise
Death's Domain
[P1] The Maimed World
Noblesse Oblige: The Crusaders
The World Hanging On Its Shadow
Rogue Humans
A Shadow Chasing A Shadow
War
Beyond The Walls Of The Universe
Actualities
True Epigones of The Sky's Son
Where Are The Sheep's Shepherds?
Innerness Awareness
Rite of Intensification
The Kerygma
And more….

TABLE OF CONTENTS

FOREWORD

May Freedom Sway Swing is a collection of poems by Ukagwu In this book, Biafra is reborn.

Of course, PE MBA UKAGWU JR. was not yet born during the Nigerian-Biafran civil war, which witnessed the deaths of over 3 million Igbos, neither did he witness the pogrom that preceded the war. However, he has, on countless times, been told stories of the war, the losses, the inhumanity visited upon his own people. He has also read books. . . books that dwelt on the short period between 1966 and 1969, when Biafra independence was declared to when the fighting Biafran soldiers surrendered to the British-backed Nigerian troop.

Aside the things he was told or things he read from books, it can be safely said that what has had the biggest impact upon an impressionable Ukagwu are the things he grew up to see and experience in his region, which falls under the then Biafra.

As one who grew up and had his education in the South-East Nigeria, he has experienced marginalization first-hand; he has seen suppression, neglect, intimidation. He has seen winds taken from visions, dreams and aspirations, as equal opportunities are denied his people.

Biafra is supposed to be God's kingdom on earth, a land of milk and honey, peopled by an uncommon kind.

The author captures these and many other experiences in May Freedom Sway Swing. The ovebearing slave master intent on perpetual subjugation of his slave; the fears and uncertainties of a future, The resolve of a people...indefatigable, undaunted, who thrive albeit laboriously.

May Freedom Sway Swing shows hope, one that can never fade.

The book is embellished with all the properties that make a great collection; good use of symbolism and imageries. The language is rich, and some times esoteric; the sound rhythmic, rhyming and and mellifluous.

Ukagwu is an Associate Member of the Academy of American Poets, and this book, May Freedom Sway Swing truly shows why he was inducted into such a prestigious Academy.

I recommend this book to all lovers of poetry and freedom, as well as all seekers of knowledge.

Charles Kaye Okoye
Editor, Book Empire Publishers

MAY FREEDOM
SWAY SWING

FREEDOM SWAY SWING

From the foundation and frame of man
Was for man found and framed,
In man was freedom in the Garden
And as air to all is free from Eden
And from none to another comes
As a due of birth, not free-for-all,

Intended by Ether inseparable be
With life as unequal boon as life,
Bosoms bullying bent in burying breaths
Before the knock knock on sepulcher
Tap, with darkened wit and intelligence
Must the rank and file of mankind
Their freedom lock away without
The key to unlock and redeem them;

Make a peep from your hidden
Submersion of treacheries that play
Against your features against mankind
O' you Judas of human tribe
And behold the divine light that
None will his freedom barter
For a sovereign sway, and all, but

Their breath will barter for freedom
Hence, give leave to upright wisdom
To rise and supersede sentiments
And jaundice and jolly your freedom
And let others their freedom jolly
That freedom in all and on all
May his airy sovereign sway swing.

HUMAN INHERENT DUE

Where shines the freedom
When the nuts and bolts
Of human inherent due
Are wanting in many a life?

When human inherent due
Are anesthetized, thus fare
Freedom, and the low live
Life of dreadful fear
In the shadowy fetid fear
From feral fermenting freedom

O' you sovereign sway swingers,
Sordid as soulless souls that
Others' congenital due must efface
Into misshapen figures in bare
Rack and ruin of beastly beating

And have their due divine
To be and breathe as Adam
In menace meanly manacled,
How long will they breathe the water
Of treachery to human genre
Remain before pierces your gloomy
Bosom the light of the sky?

Borrow this rede to have
And to hold: They that have
Their due divine in all breaths
Led by the nose but man—
And making a hash of anyone's
Takes the gilt off the gingerbread
In the fiery fangs of life's joy

All due divine lovers and admirers
Up-rouse and the cudgels take up
For they cut out of theirs
By any guise that they as you
May by their peculiar will
And wish live an airy life
As none sans such footlooseness
Owns unspurious freedom due to all.

JAUNDICE AND ANOMIA

When in the whirring procession
Of human intercourse, a field
Of carved out people of a nation
Go the vole but merely square
The circle in their free land

Crashing from rising to the fuller
Life they desire and diligent toil,
Indispensability then the travails
Earn them to melt away
From the nation if multitudinously
Congregate the desires to so do

And to stoop and scoop forces
That transform into one great
Sovereign scepter that aloft them
Stands as their singular nation -
Just as other once frozen people now
Under their peculiar nation's domes

Jaundice and anomia in societal
Air grow and diffuse as grist
For the marginalized's mill and force
For secession to the native privileges
Attain and pluck their fruits
Privileges naked in life to own

Liberty to have and to hold
The chances to reach a complete life
And swinging the state's sway
And raw privileges to them
And more in the finest way
They can when threatened own

Jaundice and anomia that put in
The shade - straining at a gnat
And engulfing a camel procure
The leavened causes for secession.

THUGGISH NATION

Where harmony and homogeneity
Hone the people and their fate
What nation raises against her
Singular seeds the massacring machines?

Such lays her unshut to her
Fractious competence in ugliness
Lynching in extrajudicial court
While courts criminal and civil
In the desuetude languish

Yet a thing glitters in a thug
Whether as an individual pate
Or a varnished nation legit
And a thuggish nation glitters
Worst in egregiousness and exhales

The most dangerous thuggish breath
No less in attitudinal wickedness
Than a tyrannical rotten corona
That tilts at windmills - what?

To have life from others' death?
To quench your power thirst
With others' running scarlet fluid?
To breathe their resigned oxygen?
To build with and upon their ruin?

SMOLDERING THE THOUGHTS

What free land smolders
The thoughts of her seeds
Before they beget utterances,
Slitting the words before
They array discernible substances?

In this civilized atmosphere
And sweet happy scented air
And mirthful hour that thoughts
Ought to joggle and jingle
As they deeply desire and salivate
And emerge and parade undreaded
As they deem fine and fit -

An inalienable privilege inherent
To all free seeds at every hour -
Peace and war, grievance and counsel
Public pother and private parley

Wise us up O' sweet land
Does your sway swing with the weight
Of the mass multitude - or
With the cannon of the despot
Against your singular seeds?

Read to us the panoply token
Of the freedom for your seeds
You flaunt your own they suckle.

HE IS NOT FREE

None who is from state affairs
Barred by marginalization or rife
Discrimination diminished of surfeit
Happenstance or by nepotistic
And tribalistic cream of the crops
Edged out of that appertained
To all - low and high, all sexes
Breathe free, nor equal to all

None who seethes in sensation
Of drought from the concatenations
Of the mouths that live off
The fat of the land - or
Breathes in nonaspirations or
In dwarfed dreams dreams
In virtue of his imprisoned estate -
Can cast the claim of being free

None who must haunt and hunt
The wild beasts without weapon
Or who must from beneath ocean
Spend hours without scuba or
Must against his grain rise
To make rendezvous of ends -
Dares whisper of being free

Unnumbered feet and minds meander
And think unfree yet seem not
Thus in their airy enclaves
But free is he who from these
Social deleterious strongholds
Shield by the sovereign sword

As all unspurious free are
When the staff sway's swirls
Into the breach for them, for
Free flourishes none sans the sway
With welfare state's alacrity
To suckle the necessitous mouths.

FRUITS OF THE THOUGHTS

Like stream stream and flow
The thoughts, and like tree twigs
The thoughts mature and bear fruits
Which by native ordinance the fructified
Tree and her fruits must without
Anomaly abide not in the tree
Nor deteriorate nor decay in
And within their better -

But leave her to rejoin the aim
For which the Unseen Force has
Enjoined them to appear
And breathe the mortal air
And nary a mortal force sans
The Sky's leave can uphold them
To the mother tree indefinite

If tree that unfamiliar breathes
Of the effigy and similitude
Of the great and glorious Sky -
Breathes free in engendering fruits -
How much more mortals with image
Of Ether stillborn the fructifying
Fruits of their thoughts! Pah!

Why mortals have it in for
Mortals, lone kakistocratic skulls
Kill the fruits of the thoughts
Ere they leave their trees
To hold forth - lest the flavor and
Fragrance settle the kakistocratic hash.

FREEDOM IN TATTERS

When the oppressors' oppression procures
Public proscriptions that hoot out
Of wincing and wailing woes
And with unspared strength for
Footloose travail with a bowed
Will to dislodge from the clutching
Claws of the grotesque specters -

No longer a momentary respite
Nor repose long they to unhitch
From the onerous heavy-hand -
As nought protracted in peace
And harmony can emerge where
Twisted nature peeps and peers -

But fain and on their toes
Stand to with expanded arms
Welcome and enfold freedom
- Albeit in tattered cassock
As an unfettered flesh forced
By Fate to feeble be to hold
A candle to fellow flesh

Fosters finest than the fettered
Flesh of preponderant air
Informuch as the dyed in the wool
Jaundiced flaws prick and pierce
To plaguing perception too profound -
More perception uprouse to the perilous
Pricking to mending fence
And papering over the cracks.

WHO IS THE JUDAS?

Who's tricked up in the gown
Of Judas and framed in his
Hovering and haunting ghost?
He who up the garden path
Unruth leads the populace

With the wave of glossed scepter;
Hence, humanity and Heaven's head,
Or she who muck-raked rabble-rouses
Or the demagogic individuals -
Standing in the fangs of the sway
That plays heaven and earth false?

Yet in virtue of his sway's sword
He swings to slay in his painted
Proclamation and presumption
Than more perfidies procure and proffer
To seal the lips of fluttered
Dovecot from uttering like their sires
Uttered and from travailing to claim

As their progenitors strove to claim,
Would also the massacring fate of their
Fearless forebears also inherit -
Bequeathed by the same high-binders
That breathed banefully and breathers
Balefully and basely exhale

As the civilized savaged slayers
And socialized serpents that they are
Striking unremorseful at anyone
Daring dauntlessly their putrefaction.

SPURIOUS AND TRUE TRAITORS

Myriads a militant rebel has
On nought been set but traitor
As his inward being is uproused
By the undiluted rawest opprobrious
Oppression piercing people's breasts,
Crashing and crushing the fences
Of virtues and humanness' pillars

Caused by the most accursed
Sincere traitors of the Adamites,
Are humans not taller than
The Magna Charta that a scarf
Of silence is on the sky cast?

The tongues skulk from the scarf
Are ferally framed traitors
And in their strike out strive
In exposing their fangs to
The true traitors of the soil
The crusading rebels labeled traitors

And as traitors are forced to
Unseen slip beneath the sod
And unsung - spurious traitors are,
Hold heart O' spurious traitors!
Soon or late, some thunderbolts
Heaped hidden in heaven, white hot

With weird indignation seething
Shall upon the oppressive high-binders
The unspurious traitors whose duty
To their land is nought but rack
And ruin in oppression, rupture.

OPPRESSION'S CONCATENATIONS

Jaundiced political misprision
In oppression and suppression swell
With the colors and forms of what
They are - unseen and unknown -
When they come to a skull
They come to where the chips
Are down - where their Concatenations
Will in the colors and forms
Familiar with them swell thus -

Where neither rewards nor punishment
Procure figures nor proffer features
But aught left beams with uglified
Effigies of eyesore consequences
Of unforeseen vicious vile -
As none takes fiery flame
To his bosom and his raiment
Remains unburned - nor the life's

Fluid not flow from flesh
Thrust with the slaying sword
Yet harmonic parley and overture
As upshots are the scarecrows
And gloom of the jaundiced
Oppressors and the beacons
And flames of the oppressed
That hapless may unknow substances.

BIAFRA ADORNED WITH SPOILS

O' Biafra! You who swell
And are with the spoils
Of Mater Nature endowed
And adorned - which have chiseled
You a soil of plunder
By alien kinfold that suckle
You dry as summer dust

And smearing across your beauty
With anguished crinkles exhibit
That sole centuries of wretchedness
And woes could lavish on forehead;

Yet so pulchritudinous nubile
You stay mesmerizing hot
As your sweet brow brighten
With your poise that its nutrients
From your hallowed hale and
Hearty huge heart stream -

A place poured and still
Pours Mater Nature hers
And her bounties bountiful
Full with respiteless and
Irretrievable munificent hand.

THE LEAST AND MOST LUMINARIES

The numerous of a state has
Since her birth nourished and
Nurtured by the phylarchy and endarcracy
 Chiseling the path of least
Antagonism for the least
Highbrowism and luminary to ride
Herd on the most highbrowism
And luminary and illustrious

Of the great glorious land;
So undemocratic viciously seems
Her in strutting her stuff
And so tyrannic and kakistocratic
Arrays she in her naked self,
The browbeating bullying beast
And the dupe and cleptobiotic
Skull and malefactor and lyncher

And leech of her peculiar people
And the bugaboo of her seeds
The very social sins she must
Smolder she shameless shines -
Her pitfalls and quicksands
Ubiquitous like a minefield
For all the luminaries that dare
Sticking the teeth of hers and

Her rottenness and rancidness;
Hence menacing sans accent
Sophisticated skulls to silence
That must grin and bear her
Kakistocracy that must dreaded
Be more than the combatant
Catastrophic crisscrossing cannons.

MONOPOLIZED POWER

Which Aboki but the cleptobiotic
High-binders, has tall above
The fences of the great land risen?
Yet you arrogate the rights
Of load-star to lead and to guide

Where is your peculiar Chinua Achebe
Or Wole Soyinka - whose both trees
Grew and still grow touching the skies
And defoliating leaves diffusing
And disseminating alow and aloft
Beneath familiar and unfamiliar
Firmaments in erudite breath exhalation?

Yet the rights of highbrowism
You arrogate to coach and drill,
Where is your singular Dick Tiger
Whose intimidating aura filled the ring
And menaced and froze his opponents?
Yet you procure the power to perform!

Where is your peculiar Fela Kuti
Whose ghost of Afro-beat still
The classic air is fraught with?
Yet you are most illustrious
Within the walls of the land!

But with the display of your deficit
To stand on your singular limbs
You trap your shame in power
Monopolized and recreating with wit
In folly every eighty-fifth person
Pauper who must as in your
Boorish hour breathe willy-nilly
From your false and flawed skills.

CARNAL FLAWS OF LIFE

Aboky, the token and carnal
Flaws of life in your turf
Have from the somber shadow
Slipped out to measure length
And heights with great Biafra —

Swinging the sovereign sway heedless
When Kismet was at your lot
One after another cleptobiotic Aboky
Came and plundered and plundered
 Until worm after worm commenced
Marched and weltered and weltered

You misremembered to mingle justice
And wisdom and clean fancies
With your soiled sway of sovereignty
In your self-serving aim when tall
You stood with seeming wreaths
Of laurels in your misgotten estate
With a magnitudes of magnificence

Albeit profound in rack and ruin
Of humanness and humility and
Worthiness, which to self-ruin slid:
A skyey stew in your singular juice

Now with glorious Biafra compared
Your current air drifts unlively life
In your semi-desert clime with boredom
And boorishness that is saturated
Sans savor of sweetness and light.

MEASURING A NATION'S GREATNESS

The love and greatness and harmonic
Oneness that entrapped a people
As a nation shine from the caring
And fosterage for the whole hearts'
Happiness enlivened indiscriminately

Leavened not by any stratification
Of color or class or creed -
But the soil's hand elongating
And her sight espying into the deep
Unknown and nameless features
By the practicality of punctilious
Policy in probity and humanness

Thus the innate skill and prowess
Untouched spurring - and promoting
Strivings, and her idiosyncratic goodwill
Must measured and weighted be
By the estate of her seeds
And the yawning and narrow chasm
Of the necessitous and opulent pates

And with a good grace stuffed
By they at the vertex to bend
An ear to pothers and grumblings
Of they seething in forgetfulness
By the sustaining sweet land

For they ever their unbroken
Fealty pay to the land -
Thriving in a witty sensitivity
And ingenious inactivity.

AFFLICTING REFLECTION

All the malevolence and misprision
That plague my heirs and heiresses
Have uprightness and civility constrained
Into the most afflicting reflection -

That, I, great and glorious Biafra,
Of too high blue-blood born
By the sacred divine thoughts
Would crashed and crushed be
To second fiddle play, and
My hash of blue-blood settled

Sole to be picked up and elevated
To useful peasant with blue
Enhued collar that cannot carry
A candle but must the candle
At the twain extremities burn
To make extremities rendezvous -

In my honey seeping land and
Milk majestic dripping mountain
And fair drifting airy space -
I in patience perdurance pure
In pain kiss pain unallayed

O' Nature! out of your shield
Shake your conscience to vigor,
Lest this non-native anomie
That in the shade put me
And knocked the spot off

My gentry by rotten skulls
That live off the fat of my soil -
Flutter the dovecotes that its
Fruit will with an unpredictable
Amorphous hysteric fury unfurl.

MY RESOLVE

I, once wounded and betrayed Biafra,
Have now my dove tongue tied
From parleying with the serpentine tongue,
My fellow feeling fettered from falling
In the crocodile's ocular waters

And my ears deafened like the adder's
To hear the bellowing of unfiltered
Whirling ululations nor the bee's buzzing
For a worm has been turning.

And aside for deleterious danger
Nor delighting delight dissolves,
My resolve to onrush proceed
As distraction slacks robust resolve
To reversion - even of the most
Noble cause of theocentric persuasion,

With a denuded heart for all
The littered kismets desiring to appease,
I proceed to pursue and persuade
With a tall pitch that pales
The pale thoughts of my rival,
Unquivering my mind and resolve stay

Informuch as firmly fixed is
The irrevocable ethereal decree
Freedom for I, Biafra, in Sky's effigy
Has to me pronounced and proclaimed,
And nary a soiled sordid soul
Can twist it nor dislodge it -
As all theocentric souls in freedom
Swell as my aim's fellow travelers.

PROCRUSTEAN FORCE

An ensemble nation they desire,
And to be - just know not they how
Nor airy in their teenie-weenie
Minds and must with Procrustean
Force force and yoke all
In one foul and unfair sordid
Soil surrounded and shredded

By all complexions of diversities -
In faiths and numberless tongues
And ancestral heritage and in
Ethos and intelligence quotient
And the seeming eternally shut
Heart to paper over the crannies
The ancient fly in the ointment

The oneness has so anomic
Grown and ever travailing striving
To reconstruct the fence cuts up
Real rough and to the quick
Severance in secession's specter
May both ways cut for all, albeit
More and less so for one and another

Yet a sight for sore sights
For the rest of the Adamic clan
For the prospect of peace it stretches
For all, uprouse and raise
Your native slumbering senses up
And your essence, that you may
Our purposes and objectives embrace.

THE POGROM SWORD

We must uprouse and divulge
To the nakedness of freedom
As the sky first tossed us into
Our peculiar climes before
The hair's breath mindedness
Of they that are in deficit
Of virtue, supplanted our freedom
Through the preference light
Of the cringing colonizers

Whose dread of our forebears'
High-browism and luminary likened
To those of the Chosen tribe
Of the Sky that was twain decades
Earlier still seething and coming up
And about from the pogrom
Unleashed for selfsame causes
And aimed to nip in the bud
Their greatness: the very menace
To they with a cut above
The remnant of Adamkind

Yes! The selfsame pogrom sword
Swung and struck and slit
And slew our sires and all
Our blood of all sexes and ages

The chips are down now
And this is the hour our ship
Arrives home for us with splendor
Like our sires sweeter it tastes
To let the scarlet stream
Unstopped streaming to the palace
Of freedom for ages that manacled
With mental manacles and momentarily
In shallowness and clouded delight
Repose in sweetness and light.

WHERE ARE THE MORAL HEROES?

Where were the moral heroes,
No! Where are the moral heroes
That ever with leaps and bounds
Lunge in the fangs of dragonish
Vices and inhumanity against humanity -
When an augmented millions
Of maters and bairns of vulnerable
And harmless Biafrans were met
By the pale horse on which rode
Demise with remorseless pogrom sword -
And lived, no, live with impunity?

Where are the arbitration of the Hague
And the International Criminal Court
That shatter and vaporize impunity
But decline to prune the grostesqueness
Of the massacring cannon welders
That stole the devil's wish
To erase the Biafran seeds?

Did not the Semitic pogrom know
Parturition in precedence and prior
To the Biafran pogrom -
Myriad of the whilom's perpetrators
And admirers and accomplices
And abetters and henchmen
Have been with poetic justice robed
In ruthless whirlwind of redress -
Hapless, nary a slight single soul
Of their Biafran counterparts has
His bitter medicine taken in any wise,

Was Genocide born when the Semitic
Pogrom rose and unruth reigned
Yet a teenager was then she
When Biafran blood indiscriminately
Spilled and soaked in her soil -
And with good hearted grace
Justice walked and still walks
Back in that anti-semitic hellish hour
To redress and right the awful vices

But knitted her sight from seeing
And so insouciant to the one
Played before her vivid view -
This disgusting shamelessness stinks
That the spheric skulls rendezvous
With the pogrom bloodbathers -
Make the spheric justice's conscience
Clean that the dread for desert
May in the bud nip atrocities.

WHAT WE OWN IN PREFERENCE

Our sires with spirits and souls
Sprang free, drilling in us
That the few in our possession
Passes the plenty in the possession
Of our oppressive cousins
Who too high price our freedom

Which shone they by playing havoc
With our oneness in severing us
With their sword of sovereignty into
Incoherent and incomprehensive states

Our fathers' feet of freedom
We will with fiery force follow
To secure that which they uproused
In us and to us deeply transmitted
And perforce make virtue
Of our inheritance and heritage
And ethereal favors and unspurious
Remain to our crystal selves -

As what we own in preference
We will to own be claiming
In the stead of what we ought
To own in preference as prescribed
By twisted-hearted heads -
The Job's comforters, proscribed by us.

NATIONS MAKE HUMANITY

Born or unborn - a nation throbs
As an enlivened organism in extant,
A breathing entity breathing robust
And as humans unlocks salubrious
Air and fancy and flowing thoughts
And running renditions ramified -
And humans her integral organs
Making ensemble of her singular self

She with other nations gathers
To ensemble and make humanity -
Hence, nations, born or unborn
Dresses to the nines as the citizens
Of humanity and under her wings
Take hide from Medusas

Just as in the airy community
Breathe humans to uphold citizenry
Of a nation invoking noblesse oblige
Of the nation to shield them -
Distraught brazenness must humanity
Bend her haloed head if incapacitated
To ward off any foul wind
Against her naked self on
Any nation - born or unborn

For worthless becomes she
If unbecoming to stake everything
To shroud and her citizens protect
In any clime where their scarlet
Water of life is running
And baking the soil with gore

As her honor shines drearier than
Her sentiments and preferences
Even than her puffed claim
Of oneness under the Adamic dome
This the pioneers and primogenitors
That one whole made humanity despised
For humans nation make
Nations humanity make.

THE ALMOST STILLBORN AND UNBORN

Does humanity by her sovereignty -
The United Nations in hypocrisy
Strive and thrive to complaisant
Be in filtering the foul
And fair affairs of nations?

Nations like humans were once
In the uterus - some still are -
Their birth and infancy had;
Some nations by Cesarean Section
Were born, others by birth labor

Yet a few almost stillborn
The Almost Stillborn there are
Still in the womb while
Humanity's midwives unconducing
Watch as they in the womb

Dysphoric with pother groaning
And moaning for the midwives
To make onrush march into the breach
With her tools for Cesarean Section
And native parturition as juncture bids

O midwives! hearken to the howls
And agonizing ululations of the babies
Intrauterine of travailing humanity
To quench the ululations gushing
From her double doubled belly

For the almost stillborn and unborn
Babies own the Sky bestowed
Divine due to be born free
And own no shush from any
Bairn of humanity - but their
Self-conscious finest choice
To engendered be by you midwives.

A COUNTRY THERE IS

"A Country There Was" quoth
An illustrious heir of the country
A country there was that by
Leaps and bounds rose high
With heirs and heiresses of great
Highbrowism and luminaries
That by ear played it

And erected her heights high
To the heavens and her aura
Vibrated all over the sphere
Weighing equipollent in currency
With the weight of British pound

And with the same full tilt
And quantum leap - equal in
Warfare with the American warriors
And industrious and indigenous scientists
Whose wrought weapons without Western
Lore nor alien condusiveness, withstood
And waged and withered her foes
And their Western wrought weapons
Ere the same Western shadows
Shadowed and endowed them with dark
Assistance to put the kibosh on her

And like a wrecked ship in the middle
Of nowhere in a torrential ocean
In a helpless agonizing distress
And like inexperienced exhausted swimmer
Descended into crevasse and sinkage
Slowly, just slowly in submission vanished
While the world with wanting worry watched

Deep, deep sank - not drown
For decades with scuba breathing
In the shadowy water beneath
And soon or late shall like
The phoenix from the pyre pile rise

And all forgetting minds will affirm
That then A Country There Was
And A Country Has Ever Been
And now A Country There Is.

FROM THE PYRE

Betimes from the pyre pile
Shall leap out and rise
And soar the great Biafra
Spreading her pietistic palms
Like the sky's curtains
Covering her climes wholly
For her singular seeds

When her oppressors in her
Parochial palace stand unseen
And powerless and lying in
Rack and ruin amidst
The Biafrans on Biafran soil

Unpeopled by the pitiless oppressors
Peopled by beaming Biafrans
With the undiminished might
And glory your light shall
As a beacon beam for many
A people all over the Adamic
Fields of tribes and races

With salubrious and solitary air
And salutary sunshine that ever
Will the hearts of they that behold
Her - warm and soothe with turbulent
Enjoyments which the bewildering
Senses will so slow be to assimilate

LET GO MY PEOPLE

You whose woolgathering has
Welded to the vow not let go -
Agitated people you resign
To let go their freedom and
Self-governance in their due
Divine from the ethereal entrails

A vanity vow of your waving
Your sovereign scepter from forgotten
Kingdom of a broken normalcy
Forswear you may not - but
Who inherit your bequeathed scepter
May his sedated skull have
Screwed in the upright way

And by diffidence or by judgment
Settle the hash of your avaricious
Ego and tyranny under one nation
Bend an ear and claim some rede:
Like the staff of the Sky
In Egypt that cried havoc:

"Let my people go" it resonates -
That their wounds cleansed
And healed be by them
And their bosom-broken blights
Be by their high-browed bosoms

Blotted away with their absolving
Indulgence pouring oil on troubled
Waters of the selfsame chests
That scourged them with sepulcheral
Aim lest like the great Pheroeh
Darkness welcomes you at
The door of infinity

MAKE A HOLY THIEVERY

Lone you like Tartarean tyrants
Trample upon others' inherent liberty
And limb from limb rend
To negate freedom framers
And fighters of their flaming
Freedom inflaming within them

Others you chisel to hereditary
Mental manacled or otherwise -
Or something worse - menticide
Lone upright hearts heartily
Cherish and cheer freedom for all

All - alow and aloft that freedom
Cherish be shaken in cheers
To share the shackles of they
Shackled by Tartarean tyrants -
As the cause of liberty cling
And to the cause of the Sky comply

Let's under the Sky's cause
Make a holy thievery of resolve
That howsoever and wheresoever
And whensoever the rally hue
And cry in ululation shrieks
In the teeth of the tyrants

For their stomping and crumpling
Freedom framers and fighters
That wanting we will never be -
That free they will leap
Over the high mortal fence
- If leap they must.

ETHEREAL BLESSED GRATITUDE

The continuum deteriorating passage
Of time that has for forgotten
Hour had the fat in the fire
Will ere pass into time out of mind
When the anomic hour arrives

Happiness and delight will claim
The bairns of the savory land,
Who borrow such hour of freedom
In their lives and will unwrap
The ethereal blessed gratitude

From their hearts - blowing them
Into every wind to volley
West and east and north and south
To all freedom loving bosoms
Conducive efforts at one fell

Swoop slashing the oppressive shackle
Yes! the blessed gratitude of bairns
Shall from shore to shore
Drift to all freedom lovers
And supporters for their theocentric

And aureate rule leavened
Noble deeds for noble cause
That tore the lips of the sky
That man has to the Sky's sacred
Desires commenced exsanguinely.

FREEDOM WARRIORS

Our forebears flaunted fervently
As liberty warriors and warlords
And were the wee few
The like lacked alow and aloft
In dauntlessness in just cause

The righteous march and procession
Which they for a season -
To view the straw in the wind - bade
A momentary farewell for peace
Piercing and harmony honing

Shelved for their nursing seeds,
Doused not the blasting furnace
Of their boiling blood for liberty -
For fight for freedom fosters
As a bequeathed inheritance

Of the green seeds once swords
Crossed and claimed years
Solely our resolve to tread
Where they trod with warriors' feet
We can hire their doughtiness.

And their dreadlessness and striking
Off the marginalized fetters
And cutting off the potentials
Restraints and the mental shackles
Shatter and the chains of second

Class citizenship to ashes burn,
To these we must with resolve
Keep firmness and set our fangs
To arrive at the skull of ours
And our great and glorious resolve:

Our primogenitors' most delightful
Dream that the sacred Chineke
Has in misremembered days
Long since sincerely stamped in
Their breasts and transmigrated to us.

SOVEREIGN SWAY AGAINST THE TONGUES AGAINST IT

The sovereign sword is feral drawn
Out of its shield to attack
And thrust and cut off and
Slaughter the tongues dancing
With veracity enhued utterances
That smirk at things too foul
To flourish and too unfair
To found be in fleshly sphere

As people's constitutional due
By greed and sway are smoldered
While nepotism and cronyism
Corruption and ethnocracy deep
Oppression in power prevail in pomp
The oppressors playing oppression
Upon the oppressed in their due
Divine while walking the line
Of the load-star of the land

The sovereign sepulchral retribution
Against the the tongues against
The sovereignty's dirty laundries
Has unshut with famished vengeance
To devour from stem to stern
In a civil sanitized air stinking
As the worn out savage age
Master-slave still swelling
Slaving the slavery skulls and
At will flinging them off
The fences of the fleshly sphere

Jaundiced justice armed with
Extrajudicial wit for lynching
Extends and spreads her grotesque
Antagonistic tentacles against her
Personae non gratae: her threats
And muck-rakers of of her ills
Scarfing the very verity voices
Of footloose constitutional due
That exhale and their disgust in
Wheezing and anguish at that which
Punctilious souls weave their brow at

Straight from the shoulder accents
Show the universal constitutional due
That grace a people pettling their
Tongues if free society that in concord
Pettles her free people unbiased
As none without his opinion to lend
To his tongue for and against society's
Ills can over sepulchered slavery gloat
Hence all must their opinions be
Permited to pour in and paint society
As she sincerely on hers' reflects

For this' a due divine dazzling
Which lofty superior precious and
Panoply passes peace in plenty
Uncaging the innermost man confined
In cloud of chaos of carte blanche
Liberating of all from fear of tyranny
And levitating them to the heights
Of options and opinions to proceed
In procession amidst the pillars
Of the due divine of Adamic dignity.

WHEN BY FREEDOM SUCKLED

The uncharted hour with swift
And full tilt rolling-wheels rolls
Bringing with it the gift of Heaven
That will with winds so salutary
And salubrious usher us into
Sweetness and light in equal waves
Of chances and welfare for all

And the shield for the nuts
And bolts of humanness and
Inherent inheritance of life
As heirs and heiresses of humanity
And own the surging sensations
Of their airy weight in eyrie
Of mental unshackled free life

And in the greenish air -
As all the joie de vivre thrive
True and sturdy when by Freedom
Suckled inasmuch as sole unaffected
Minds foster airy burning breaths
And prolong breaths that pass medium

What a nobility glows salubrious
Freedom that endows all diverse
Likings and absentmindedly tosses
Them in the lair of sweetness
And light that they may at
The eyrie of easement live
And unscarfed freely live it!

PRESCRIBED PRECEPTS

Every people though mixed minds
But with semblance of ethos
And hallowed heritage enrich
Merit and qualification with skyey
Sanction to gain and garner
Humanity's heart and head and
Hand to pull independence' chestnuts
Out of the blasting furnace

If and when the sensation
They have at one with all
And profoundly so desire it -
For a Moses-staff and lodestar
They deserve which will every apparition
Warrant the thoroughgoing trimmed
Civilized instinct of due of birth
In nakedness with footlooseness

As he pleases breathes and the whirlwind
Of how he breathes reaps within
The synthesized sympathetic pale
Upon the ubiquitous privileges,
Elevating the people aloft the Corona
In chiseling out salutary loadstar
From aloft the cerulean sky
Bestowing them obstreperous will

To follow the peculiar will -
Partially passive and partially intransigent
In everything in rendezvous
Of minds of the prescription and
Proscription of the precepts and power
Solely the salutary goodwish of power
For its subjects and its fail
Deference to their footlooseness can

This attain and incur their deference
In obsequious obeisance for the sway
For when a people ascend in descending
In self-governance - a prescribed precept
For themselves they beseem -
The true practicality of their ethos
That pours oil on troubledwaters
In the air if the fat be in the fire.

BIAFRA - A MULIER

Biafra is the hovering thoughts
And glory and grandeur
Of the ethereal Supreme Head
Made flesh in mulierty - a mulier

A filial heiress sweet and zaftig
With mulierbrity air and fair
As heiress of Eve, of Eden
Could ever fair seem

Heiress assiduously robust
For salubrious labor and seeming
After her knitting as salutary
Adamic bona fide heiress

Could pay airy heed to;
Holding the line given to
The human begetters that rung
Up the curtain on humanity

Cut out for noblesse oblige
As the glorious Biafra
That reposes in sweetness
And light and overwrought

To hail-fellow-well-met be
In hospitality to strangers
From unfamiliar firmaments
The pride of the tribe
Of the Adamite - shine on!

HAIL-FELLOW-WELL-MET

When the final strike on
The camel's back strikes
To etch the bounds of Biafra
From the entity Nigeria -
Biafra hail-fellow-well-met
To her still retains in mind
And thoughts and renditions

Being thus to her green
Neighbor to scarf her scars
From the massacre ventured,
As she with a good grace
To love all housemates
Beneath the Adamic dome,
Must ever her verdorous
Neighbor love unblighted,

Unbonneted that the halcyonic
Zephyr may to and fro the modern
And ancient wend and wander -
That the gloomy cumuli -
May far far away fade

And aurora sun of Biafra
Surmounting the bowing horizon
To summerly shine upon
The stripling soil and verdant

Leaves of our airy lives -
While she stretches her honest
Hand to good neighborliness
And friendship and fine rapport
Across the great Niger River.

BIAFRA'S SPLENDOR

O glorious Biafra! to your splendors
You shall at nick of time
Raise and stand as the prince
Of the orbit and the favored
Bairn of the great Above -
When the crown of patience
And perseverance in parleys
Shall upon you crowned be

When the diadem of freedom
Shall upon you panoply rest
When the regal raiment
Of victory you array
And in panoply pomp
Parade you in high jinks

When the doves of your resolve
Shall the air fill comely
Their feathers settling on your hat
When your clime the sincere
Soil of no slavery disguised
Be but all breathing your air
Egalitarian in every intercourse
With none so much the most
Nor any so much the least

Where no predator prowls
And preys any hapless prey
The heights of your splendor
I espy not, but your splendor
Shall from all round the rounding
Be seen in reverence unknown
At the nick of the bright hour -
When time shall at the skull
Of our delightful hope arrive.

WHAT A GREAT LOVE!

O' you brave bosoms of Biafra
Who malleable bent your will
And staid stayed unwearied
For the state of uterine Biafra
Chivalrous with ancient warrior's
Resolve and bravery burning bosom

For her freedom fain to unleash
Your blue-blood and breaths
For her you bled and beheld
Ghoulish black Death riding
On her pale horse with her
Reaping sickle of massacre

Massacring every hapless sex
Every hapless age - remorseless;
Solely the Sky under tbe shadow
Of his pinions had shielded you
That the languishing longing
Of Biafra you might uphold

And her flame of freedom
Keep blazing unquenchable -
With fervent love loving her
Ere her birth was dawned
For what she in the womb
Was and what would be she -
What a great love showed!

GLORIOUS BIAFRANS

In our fearless forebears' loins
We as Biafrans had fought
If the dust they had bitten
We would have selfsame had

Bitten the bullet as did they
Our bit to do deep deeply
And our lone end to wreathe
A wreath of laurels and set
Her to repose upon it

Making her glorious round
And glorious to be in her
Glorious to halcyonic breath
In her and weaned by her

Glorious to go to glory
For her - elevating us more
Dyed in the wool bona fide
Biafrans we were in those
Days blood-curdling spectral,

Glittering us selfsame glorious
As our crusading ancestors
Lived Biafrans crusading undread
And went to glory Biafrans.

WITH ALCHEMICAL ALACRITY

The youngest of the world
Ancient nations has finally
From bondage set to liberty
Hurling away the shackles
That pinioned her panoply pinions
Rending the crape hemming her
Style on a samber mountain
Of decades and centuries

Now by leaps and bounds
As in the antique day onrush
Commences she with alchemical
Alacrity tied about herself
To play by ear in the juncture
Of her singularity, by strivings

And to catch a tartar in
The orbicular orbiculating juncture
With flaming confidence yanked
From the firmaments rolling you
Into the bright uncreated days -
Where espy l you in virtue and
Fairness of tales of our sires

Of your ethos and pathos ancient
And your sway swinging in swell
Not at our due of parturition
Of singular judgment in issues
Of conscience, nor other basic
And shadow of your pinions
That have vaulted your skies
To shadow your brood as a hen

None can curb nor curtail
Your confidence nor your enhued
Aspiring breath and inuttero days
Sans tyranny shall stand sway unswaying.

ONE SELFSAME NATION

The succulent sovereign tree
Of the Biafra soil under
The lore and ethos of democratic
Tribes shall fructify her
Constitutional fruits with its flavorous
Authority must from the people's
Savorous consent and assent
Teem and full be derived

Blindfolded in protecting all
Her bairns in fructifying liberty
All - low and high equal eating
And drinking the entitlements
Of delectable deserts from her
Constitutional nourishing sustenance
Of liberty and justice and all
Rights basic that none may no
Severed allegiance beholden to her

As one nation of selfsame soil
Selfsame hope and selfsame flag
And selfsame constitution under
Selfsame dome shading and shielding
All indiscriminately as one with
Selfsame unshackled chances
Nutritiously nourishing social justice
To all: one selfsame nation to all.

GRATULATED PRAISES

May all blue-blood Biafrans
Raise gratulated praises
To overhead the cerulean
Ether - shake the lilies
Of delight and toss
The aureate dust of glory
Aloft the ethereal dome

The substances of our dazzling
Dust of delight decorate
And display our guise interior
Under our contemporary sun
The beauty and grandeur
Of the land's greatness
Swell to be seen crystal

And our arrows and shots
Of petitions flying and hitting
Above the blue firmaments
Where they everywhen abide
At one with our appreciative praises.

BIAFRA'S DAWN DAWNING

Arrayed in fair as the sunrise
As she dresses to the nines
As true regal warlord - the great
Biafra that engendered her gallant
Warriors that engendered her -

Just as the Tongue of Ether
Has deep in the wool dyed
The apodictic truism: "Woman
From man knew existence and
Man from woman knows existence"

With unknown harmony and unity
Stoops her to raise all the rabble
Misremembered in the heap of rubble
Of social ostracism and economic
Marginalization - stoops her to soothe
The seething and sooty soil
And glorify her dawning dawn

Flee all you specters of imbroglios
To the black breast of oblivion
From her halcyonic heart and
Luminary and high-browed womb -
Lest any of her heirs or heiresses
Of Hitlerite hate hypnotized be

May pyrrhic victorious liberty
Glorify her warriors as her
Warriors fiery fair and fervent
Free hail freedom upon that
Biafra flaunts and flouts at
High-handed scoundrel sovereignty

To sweetness and light her
Ethereal endowed flavored
Favors her bairns coalesce -
Augmenting their synergistic
Prowesses and selflessness
And unnationalistic patriotism

All-out - enriching her huge heart
With probity and punctiliousness
So plenty to apportion to all
Her rich goodness with airy
Theocentric laced policy protect.

CHEERS OF INDEPENDENCE

Cheer and cheer for the aurora
Of Independence has to the skull
Come - with her fiery charms
Of scouth blessings tossed by
Elohim - even in the local climes

Let Independence our cheer airy
And tempestuous be in the air -
Leaving the flames of memory
Burn in the sacrifices that wrought
And begotten her sweet self
And igniting the hearth of gratitude

For and to all the lips that kissed
The dust and limbs and other
Members missing in action
From our heroic sires days to ours
As befitting abundance it thrives
To without revelry revel and cheer

At her altar than with all royal
Pomp and cannon of twain
Tens and one greetings at the court
Of anniversary of masquerade
Of civilized servitude and scoundrel

Let to the sky our cheer for her
Echo unending as the hallowed
Hand of Heaven essence granted
Her in our intra mundane day

Let the children's cheerful cheers
And onrush innocence enshroud
And warm her - for every dream
Will actuality claim and every aspiration
Appearance - for the marginalizing

Lines have been blotted crystal
With nary a fencing line and unseen
Fences that kept and barred
Man from man and warded off
Gregariousness and hobnobbing.

ALL AS INTEGRAL ENSEMBLE

All with selfsame weight of
Connaturalness of the land
 In equipollent scale - none
Owning nor claiming less
Or more in deserving or
Undeserving - as none than
Others more worthy nor
Any than others less worthy

None too common
None too uncommon
None dynastic or undynastic
Privileged - none with trimmed
Opportunities - all with wild
Opportunities and chances

None with dispensed heart
Or mind - all with their singular
Heart and mind - each with
Their undomesticated talent
Each integral and none integer

All assembled as inseparable
Ensemble - as any integral
Grief and burden and plague
Integrate the ensemble -
The ensemble standing
The good the stead
Of the integral clime
With the integral streaming
Strength of the others.

LOYAL TO THE BLOOD

Heaven streaming strength into
The breach will swirl onward
To proffer you a hand O' Biafra
To in freedom fight redeem
Restrained rights and liberty
For all your precious brood

For Biafra's bravery shall
The Biafran wrong be righted
That Biafra's blood may not
Bleed away by the compression
Of oppression and high-binders

The unborn eras as bequeathed
Shall the chiseled out liberty
By the sires' blood and bravery
Inherit with unspared strength
And sustain - as to it's being loyal

To the blood flowed and
The gorest soil soiled by
Pogrom - all must the spectral
And sepulchral chance of loss
And disaster absorb and hold

BIAFRA'S PRIDE AND SPLENDOR

Behold beautiful Biafra in her
Probity tricked out in glittering
Evergreen - eternal verdant dress
She whose pride and splendor
Lie not upon cannon
Like superpowers - but upon
The omnipotence of hers
And her airy ethos and pathos

Peerless amidst her peers
Invigorating vigors of her
Humanness and savoir-vivre
Upon you O Biafra fall
More than a million million
Starry favors the Sky
Through the entrails of Nature
By maternal indulgence could
Be benevolent with and to
A people thus blessed as yours.

ANCIENT BIAFRANS STALKS

Among that that Heaven unto her
Proffered with a prodigal finger
Her heiresses and heirs - hapless
Princesses and princes void of
Their birth inheritance and comeliness
In their ethereal soil of scouth

Yet sui generis mould of interiority
And of ancient Biafrans stalks -
A people of no mean minds -
Vaunt if it be vaunted that
Nary a sibship there swells in
Scintillation as ours in any stripe

Nor any hospitality its boisterous
In intensity wounds with kindness
As ours in our inward climes
Where those scorched with our
Reception creep out of their demure
Selves to coalesce with us unabased

Which sparks the fire in true Biafrans
Even in the gloomy bottomless chasm
Never to be roused with revolving
Thoughts nor wish to be any other
Stalk than a Biafran - even in hell

For a Biafan of all Adamites will
Uphold the Eternal steamy yearning
And sacred scepter of fellow feeling
A substantial substance of Sky's semblance.

TO THE PRIME CHIEF OF BIAFRA

I have with obeisance bent my knees
As l borrowed the revered liberty to hail you
Your Excellency in the cloak colorful voiceless accent
Their acceptance I beseech you make
For from the seraphic seas of the Sky stream them
You have by dainty levitated by well-meaning
Salubrious and salutary yearning
Heads with huge hearts to the overlord
Of this great glorious land be -
Unanimously with a warriors renown -
With a feather in your glittering hat
Ignited fire of joy - a Herculean toil
To extinguish - in my breast burns
After the manner of overwrought fragrance
As l swear is ebullient in your breast too
As well as multitudinous other chests.

In awe espy l the seraphic symphonies
Swallowing hellish wishes that hovered
Over Chukwu Okike's Land on earth -
With clasping cymbals and trumpets -
Trumpeting sounds singing and swinging -
Dancing in the skyey seas of jamboree
And jubilation that the skyey Scepter has
His great Land snatched from fiends -
Cheating the Devil and his retinue -
Even a whit of his taking the hindmost
Of it the high handed heads and hearts
That proved square pegs in round holes.

The prime dripping of honey from Canaan
I blaze the good tidings of sight for sore eyes.
While wearied the Land trudged
From boring shots times five
From feeble brain fatigues
Whose usurpations rounds through her
Breast spot pierced and by the dwarf
Hair grabbed in intervals by multitude
Avaricious fingers for too long
That giddily strode she in the spheric affairs
Took, which to a counterfeit demise lulled her

But today whirls the healing wind
Of her intolerable wounds and bruises
At the commence of you and your wits
Like the cat that engulfed the canary she looks
And multitudinous causes she owns
For such ecstatic glowing rupturous joy and hope:
For fair justice and true freedom shine
With cheering delight like mid of summer -
No more shall venality and other malfeasances
Glow with rife in this divine flavorous favored Land
Advancements shall against stagnations rise
Feasible privileges transforming to peculiar successes
That shall savagely drag rack and ruin to crime
With these in happen-stance power and character
The lofty log that many heads pull down
From their enthusiasm and strives to scale
Virtue standing upon the decadence of office -
All at the summit of scientific lore arrive
And shall shatter in shambles ignorance
In multitudinous pieces too tiny to perturb -
All from mental darkness be bought out

The Land's goddess flaunts in proud
Pomp and gracely strides in divine delight
For the Eternal's dainty has disjoined her
From her battening adopted sister - adjudged
The great Land's throne with limitless ray
Of shining for her dark paths and all her plains
Today's set for her immortal monumental glory
To glow as proud as any sea of its swirling
Waves and any great downpour of its flood
Who can the ugly hand raise to spike your gun?
None! Even the fainting pessimists say thus
Yet upon you the green kismet of this great
Glorious Land rides. - to another Doom or Glory -
More moaning and groaning
Or surging of joy and happiness

Hence to her favor or against it lies
In your hand to load the fateful dice
For whichever that in your lot finds easement
Shackles her to the bailiwick of graces
Of good and bad of her glorious greatness
Which will her wistful head sagged
Or her strength shall sans fatigue hurdle and fly
While her wits at the boughs of the skies perch
All moans are by the glowing hope scarfed
Yes! bosoms are burning with irresistible joy
That from profound prospect surges beyond experience
Profound prospect that with flame of optimism sears
The optimism that from deep confidence sprang
The confidence that has its brawn anchored
In who Biafra is and her divine beliefs
Of moral supremacy of Life - top full

O' your Excellency! heads without number
Have their prospect and optimism unshackled
To fly and soar without retreat
Nor tear of regret for choicing you
As having the courage of their conviction -
Mind over issue they prevailed that :
They were on the erroneous stallion not betting
Nor were they on the erroneous tree barking
But sans a grain of salt swallowed all
The utterances hewed from your manifesto:
A covenant of faith and of trust

Thus like the lizards that after their nocturnal confabulation
The night before solely acknowledge one
And another in the day by nodding at one with all
Indeed, to their minds and not misknowing
Their peculiar minds, fished and cut bait
That you and lone you owned merit their bosoms
To point the moonbeam for their feet

In these lavender fragrant scented accent
Your great indulgence will delicately absolve
My gene fleeting hot-blooded Biafran blood I adjudge
May all the summed Forces from aloft the Firmaments
By the sacred tongues of your fellow heirs
And heiresses and princes and princesses
Of this great kingdom enliven all the virtues
Indispensable to carry her to Redemption Land
Encircle your unctuous head, and every rendition
Ascends and descends the skyey seas
Of seraphic delight that will bide in you
Your manege and all seeds of this great Land
All to this and awaiting generations
And may these scented electrified lines
From age to age transmigrate to favored heads
That will the great glorious corona carry
In the precinct and promenade of her pride promenade
And your name as the prime grandeur
In the scroll of this Land's greatness stand

My sacred tongue and others' of sacred
Thoughts raise our sanctified wishes
To the boisterous but jubilating Sky
For you and our glorious entity Biafra
That you will far far away fan
Every dust of misery and misease
From every heart and multitudinous bosoms
Hail! Hail!! Hail!!! the Prime Chief
Of the great people of great Biafra!
For today begotten is the sui generis soil
With bairns of uncommon savoir vivre.

SWORN ALLEGIANCE

With sworn allegiance to uphold
Tributary to the sovereignty of Biafra
With an ebullient passion
For perfection in loyalty and performance
With mind widen with imaginations
To stay her victory, harmony
And freedom in faithfulness
In defense of her constitution
And enforcement of her duty
At all time - l will.

BRUCE MAYROCK : AN IDEALIST AND ZEALOT
MAY 6, 1949 - MAY 30, 1969

Mayrock - sui generis idealist and zealot,
Great martyr of conscience and justice
A nonself annihilation it was
But fain caught the atrocious pogrom
Callousness and cannon of salvoes
Aimed at Biafra's undying breath

Like the Deliverer of earth
That his breath doffed off
For his friends - the greatest
Love of all loves, thus was yours
Its blaze in all Biafrans burns still

.